IS THE FAMILY
HERE
TO STAY?

IS THE FAMILY
HERE
TO STAY?

David Allan Hubbard

WORD BOOKS, Publisher

Waco, Texas

CONTENTS

Introduction

Criticism of present-day family life is coming from all sides. This past year almost every major news magazine carried feature articles on the family. Titles like, "Is the American Family Obsolete?", "The American Family: Future Uncertain," and "Can the Family Survive?", reflect the intense concern felt nationwide. Television and radio have broadcast "specials" dealing specifically with the family. The United States government has established task forces to investigate problems within the structure of today's families.

The problem becomes more critical every day. Marriages are breaking up; children are running away from home. One marriage in three ends in divorce. In some West Coast communities the divorce rate is 70 percent. Every year an estimated one-half million children run away from their families. The problems facing the family today have reached epidemic proportions.

Where do we turn for help? Magazines, newspapers, committee reports, and electronic media offer good analyses. They pinpoint the problems, but they are hard pressed to offer solutions for their words carry no power to change human lives. There is not a news commentator or journalist living today who would stand up and say, "Listen to me and your life will be changed."

But that's exactly what the Bible does say. Where then should we turn for help? To the God of the Bible. To the beliefs, guidelines, ministries provided for the chosen people, the family of God. The Bible has important lessons which can help us through the crisis period. In both the Old and New Testaments we see how truly important the family is in God's program.

Early Israel was neither a racial nor a national unit. It was a confederation of tribes (families) united in a covenant with Yahweh. The twelve tribes of Jacob (Israel) were an external expression of Israel's covenant faith with God. In Israel, beliefs were important. A man's knowledge of himself and his relation to his wife, children, and neighbors hinged on his relationship with God.

Guidelines were necessary. The very nature of a covenant or contract stipulates some concept of law. For the covenant people there were and are covenant regulations.

Ministry was vital. The people of God were chosen for a life of ministry. Ministry among themselves and to others. It was through the family of Israel that the world's Savior came. It was for this purpose that they were "chosen."

In the New Testament Christ teaches that corporate life for his disciples should be patterned after the family. When Christ taught his disciples to pray he began his prayer, "Our Father ..." (Matt. 6:9).

The Apostle Paul when writing to the Ephesians also

8

stressed the central character of the family in God's ongoing program. To God our family relationships are so vital that the very nature of the family originates with him (Eph. 3:15).

The family's importance is elevated throughout the Bible. In Ephesians 5 and 6 the Apostle Paul outlines our family relationships in great detail. The family has a supreme example—Jesus Christ. As the church is subject to Christ so wives ought to be subject to their husbands. As Christ loved the church so ought the husband to love his wife. Parents are to instruct and discipline their children. Children are to obey their parents. Make no mistake about it, the pattern for family life is important to God.

It is important to God what your family believes. The relationships between husband and wife, parents and children hinge on belief in the lordship of Christ (Eph. 5).

What guideline does your family follow? Is your starting point the Word of God? We are all called to be "obedient children" of our Father in heaven (1 Pet. 1:14). God's rules are strategic for healthy family relationships.

Does your family live for service? Is ministry your aim? Our families should be mirrors of God's unending love and patience. In our life together we should reflect our membership in the family of God. Our call to service is high because our Father is a king. God entered into the mainstream of humanity through a family. He wants to use your family also.

THE BELIEFS
OF THE FAMILY

1

Are Marriages Made in Heaven?

Then God said, "Let us make man in our image, after our likeness; and let them have dominion over the fish of the sea, and over the birds of the air, and over the cattle, and over all the earth, and over every creeping thing that creeps upon the earth." So God created man in his own image, in the image of God he created him; male and female he created them. And God blessed them, and God said to them, "Be fruitful and multiply, and fill the earth and subdue it; and have dominion over the fish of the sea and over the birds of the air and over every living thing that moves upon the earth." And God said, "Behold, I have given you every plant yielding seed which is upon the face of all the earth, and every tree with seed in its fruit; you shall have them for food. And to every beast of the earth, and to every bird of the air, and to everything that creeps on the earth, everything that has the breath of life, I have given every green plant for food." And it was so. And God saw everything that he had made, and behold, it was very good. And there was evening and there was morning, a sixth day.

1

Are Marriages Made in Heaven?

Genesis 1:26–31

Marriage as an institution is under sharp attack. From many sides barrages are being leveled at our practice of living permanently with the same partner.

Young people call marriage unsatisfactory and hypocritical. Why should they endure decades of bickering and badgering just for the sake of convention? Why pretend to stoke the coals of love when the fire has obviously gone out?

If we suggest that the family should stick together for the sake of the children, the younger generation may retort: "Who wants to be raised in a home where the parents break the stony silence only to yell at each other? What kind of a favor is it to rear children in the midst of a battlefield?"

While some of our young people are battering marriage from without, many of us older folks are undermining it from within. We urge that marriage is essential, a God-ordained institution for the welfare of the human family; then we devote almost no time or energy to making marriage work. We pay lip service to

15

the home as the foundation of our society, and then proceed to neglect it by our preoccupation with business or social activities.

What's at stake in this massive assault on marriage is not just the question, "Did I marry the right partner?" It's the deeper issue: "Is marriage itself worthwhile? Is the family here to stay?"

On every side we hear the discontent. Popular songs celebrate short, passionate, and fleeting affairs. Internationally known personalities have children out of wedlock. Movie stars live together and make no bones about their fear of marriage: "We have such a beautiful relationship now, but we're afraid marriage will spoil it."

This disparagement of marriage is contagious. Thousands of university students have learned to be promiscuous and to deceive themselves into enjoying it. In most of our large cities there are apartments where young professionals (single and divorced) live together, desperately trying to savor the pleasures of marriage without shouldering its responsibilities.

Where once we talked about marriages being made in heaven, now we're not sure that marriage can even be endured on earth. For some, marriage is too boring: "How dull to spend all of one's life with one person." For others, marriage is too confining: "I want to come and go as I please. Don't fence me in. Too much responsibility gets me uptight."

Decisions to be made, bills to be paid, children to be raised, compromises to be worked out, plans to be changed—marriage is made of stern stuff. Adjustment, concern, and sacrifice cause plenty of people to wonder if marriage is really worth it.

16

Is the family here to stay? This is the question we want to lay bare. You will be surprised to see how much the Bible has to say about marriage and the family. For one thing, the Bible makes the tightest possible connections between its central themes and the place of marriage in God's program. From beginning to end—from the creation of man as male and female to the climax of God's saving work at the wedding supper of the Lamb—marriage is thrust into prominence by the men who heard God's Word and recorded it.

With our Bibles open in front of us, we will look at some of the questions that arise whenever men and women discuss marriage seriously. Is till death do us part too long a time? Is marriage for better or for worse? Does father know best? How can we treat children like people? How can families be friends?

Are marriages made in heaven? This question pops up frequently in discussion sessions with young adults. And it's a good one to begin with because it brings to the forefront the relationship between marriage and the will and plan of God for human life.

Our Capacity for Marriage

We must begin at the beginning—or to be more exact, five days afterward. The first five days of creation set the stage: day and night, waters above and waters below, sea and dry land, vegetables and fruit trees, a bright light for day and a subdued light for night, birds and fish. The environment was ready. The arena was set up. Day six dawned and God created the animals and the reptiles. Then the climax: *"God said, Let us make man in our image, after our likeness; and let them have dominion over the fish of the sea . . . and over all the earth, and over every creeping thing that creeps . . . upon the earth"* (Gen. 1:26).

No sooner said than done, because God is speaking: *"So God created man in his own image, in the image of God he created him; male and female he created them. And God blessed them . . ."* (Gen. 1:27–28).

Among other things, this magnificent account of our human beginnings lays the foundation for our understanding of marriage. Man is the pinnacle, the crown of God's creation. Everything that takes place before prepares the way for man's appearance. And as soon as man appears and gets his instructions from God, God rests, his creative work completed.

And man, this masterpiece of God's creation, much more like God than anything else in the world, is male and female: *"In the image of God he created him; male and female he created them."*

In other words our capacity for marriage is God-given. Our physical nature with its masculine and feminine characteristics was fashioned by God himself. This, of course, does not mean we can blame him for all the foolish or frightful things we do with our bodies. It does mean that our maleness and femaleness—our basic sexuality—are gifts of his love and grace.

All of us know that masculinity and femininity are more than physical traits. Our emotional make-up is tied closely to our maleness and femaleness. The way we feel, reason, respond, relate, is part of our being male and female. Little boys react differently from little girls to their experiences. Parents merely have to discuss a sensitive issue like money, clothes, or politics to know that male and female feelings are not the same. And they shouldn't be. God made us different so that we can support and complement each other.

Whether every marriage is made in heaven or not is a difficult theological question that engages us in the issue of God's sovereignty and how it applies to life's decisions. But we can be sure that marriage itself is divinely commissioned. God went to great lengths to equip us to make marriage the chief social institution of our lives.

Our Purposes in Marriage

God has not left us to guess why marriage is so important. The Bible stresses at least three purposes which God had in mind when he endowed men and women with the capacity for marriage.

First, he was committed to the continuation of the human race. *"Be fruitful and multiply and fill the earth and subdue it"* was the first demand the Creator made of the brand new man in the beginning (Gen. 1:28). God wanted a race, a people, a vast human family to make his name known and to make his glory clear throughout the earth. Marriage, with the bearing and rearing of children, was his way of making this possible.

God's second purpose in establishing marriage was our enjoyment of a relationship. *"It is not good,"* God declared, *"that the man should be alone"* (Gen. 2:18). Through all the previous stages of creation God's evaluation had been positive: *"And God saw that it was good"* (Gen. 1:4, 10, 12, 18, 25, 31). Here's the first negative note: "not good," not in keeping with my purpose and intent; not what I had in mind when I made man.

Relationship is what life is all about. Even God lives in relationship—Father, Son, Holy Spirit—three persons, one God. And one of the ways that man is like God is that he is capable of knowing, loving, revealing himself to, and learning from another person, a person like him.

Animals are not enough, the man found out when God made them and brought them to him for naming. But when God brought the woman, the man's exuberance was unbounded: *"This at last is bone of my bones and flesh of my flesh"* (Gen. 2:23). He's almost singing his excitement. He sees their similarities and differences and rejoices in both.

The enjoyment of the relationship—physically, emotionally, spiritually—is so important in our marriages that God has placed a book in the Scriptures that deals exclusively with this theme: the Song of Solomon. Read it at your leisure, and sense the beauty and power which can radiate from a marriage that is turned-on to God's purposes.

But God has an even deeper purpose in view when he calls us to enjoy the fellowship of our marriage partners—the demonstration of divine love. Marriage is an object lesson, an illustrated sermon whose text is John 3:16: *"God so loved the world that he gave . . . "*

What God had in mind more than anything else, when he ordained marriage and gave us such high potential to enjoy it, was that we should love each other as husbands and wives so constantly, fervently, and responsibly that all who see our love would be reminded of his. *"Husbands, love your wives, as Christ loved the church and gave himself up for her"* (Eph.

5:25). This is Paul's straightforward summary of Christ's costly commitment to his church.

How does your marriage compare with the Bible's picture? How do your purposes in marriage check with God's? Marriage is made in heaven. But unless we are tuned in to God's plans our individual marriages can be hell on earth—steeped in selfishness, corroded with hostility, encrusted with bitterness, and explosive with lust.

Committing your life to God is not an instant solution to all your problems. But it is the first step in finding out what your marriage really can be. God ought to know. He's the founder of the institution, and he still believes in it as firmly as he ever did.

PRAYER: Father, we know that comparisons can be odious, but sometimes they can be profitable as well. We have compared our experience with your plan, and we have found ourselves at a loss. Save the marriages that are now being battered on the rocks of selfishness and misunderstanding. Strengthen the marriages that are sagging under the pressures of emotional, financial, and sexual problems. Father, show your love in Jesus Christ to all who taste little but trouble, whose hopes have turned to gall in the sourness of life. You who are Father and Husband to your people, teach us the delights of your love. Through Jesus Christ, who loved us and gave himself for us. Amen.

For further study on the importance of marriage, refer to the following Scripture passages: 1 Corinthians 7:9–11; Hebrews 13:4; 1 Timothy 4:1–5.

2

Is "Till Death Do Us Part" Too Long a Time?

The man gave names to all cattle, and to the birds of the air, and to every beast of the field; but for the man there was not found a helper fit for him. So the Lord God caused a deep sleep to fall upon the man, and while he slept took one of his ribs and closed up its place with flesh; and the rib which the Lord God had taken from the man he made into a woman and brought her to the man. Then the man said,

"This at last is bone of my bones
and flesh of my flesh;
she shall be called Woman,
because she was taken out of Man."

Therefore a man leaves his father and mother and cleaves to his wife; and they become one flesh.

2

Is "Till Death Do Us Part" Too Long a Time?

Genesis 2:20–24

"Nothing but a scrap of paper—that's what a marriage license is!" This kind of extravagant statement is a symptom of the spirit of our age. With increasing frequency marriage is being put down, cast aside, overturned.

So-called meaningful relationships are placed at a premium, and permanent marital commitments are depreciated. The wedding ceremony may still contain the words "so long as ye both shall live" or "till death do us part," but they are viewed as poetic license, exaggerated expressions of the concern the bride and groom feel for each other at this moment.

At this moment is the key because it is the now generation that is of an age for marrying. To them next year seems a lifetime away, and "till death do us part" is too long a time to contemplate.

If our young people find it hard to take marriage seriously, we don't have to look far for the reason.

Their parents haven't won Nobel Prizes for high achievements in the field of matrimony. The children have been anxious spectators at many a family brawl. They know something of vows that have been flagrantly broken or grudgingly kept. Many of them have been moved in the night like gypsies as their homes have dissolved and their parents separated.

If they go through the formalities of marriage, it is as a reluctant conformity to convention or a ceremonial sop to parental anxiety. Their marriage license is nothing but a scrap of paper. Like vagabonds they may roam from relationship to relationship, from lustful lark to sordid exploitation. And all the time they try to reassure themselves that this irresponsibility is a new form of freedom.

They even sing about it. A lonely, lost waif of a girl tells her lover that they'll live light and easy for a while and then she'll leave. She warns him against deep involvement because she's not prepared for permanent commitment.

A wedding license? A scrap of paper! But wait a minute. Aren't scraps of paper important? Is it not one of the marks of civilized men that they protect themselves against their savagery by scraps of paper? Sure a wedding license is a scrap of paper, but so is an employment contract, your pay check, a twenty-dollar bill, the deed to your home, the Constitution of the United States.

The Possibilities of Permanence

The wedding license is one way of showing that marriage is intended to be permanent. The possibilities for this permanence are pictured in the earliest wedding portrait ever taken. The camera of Genesis catches Adam and Eve at the moment of their first meeting.

Adam is overwhelmed by the close affinity that he senses with this woman. She is like him. But even more she is part of him: *"This at last is bone of my bones and flesh of my flesh"* (Gen. 2:23). The woman was different from the trees of the garden which offered their ample fruit, different from the animals whose traits and habits Adam had dutifully noted when he named them. The woman was his kind—open to communion, capable of fellowship, ready for affection.

He saw her as a person, a living self with all the rich potential that he sensed in himself. She was not a tool to be used in the tilling of the garden nor a toy to be played with in the cool of the evening, but a person to be loved, honored, respected.

No need for boredom here because she's a person, made in God's image, capable of wonderful thoughts and beautiful feelings, able to learn, to grow, to mature, to respond. An uncanny, uncommon kind of partnership is possible. God made it so, and Adam sensed it immediately.

This partnership has the possibility of permanence not only because of the close affinity between the man and his wife but also because of the rich diversity. In that first wedding portrait the bride wore no gown and the groom no tuxedo: *"And the man and his wife were both naked, and were not ashamed"* (Gen. 2:25). Open to the gaze of both of them were their physical differences. And these physical differences were evidence of differences of mind and soul, of feeling and attitude, of perspectives and insights.

They could respond to each other because they were alike—both human beings. They needed each other because they were different—neither complete without the other. Two able to be one. Truly one because they were two. Permanent relationship was possible, built into the very stuff of which they were made. *"Therefore,"* is God's conclusion, *"a man leaves his father and his mother and cleaves to his wife, and they become one flesh"* (Gen. 2:24).

The Importance of Permanence

This gluelike loyalty which God made possible in the way he created us is important for several reasons. Socially, a permanent relationship between parents is important to the welfare, stability, and nurture of the children. God is forming a people; children are important to his program. He has not left them to grow up like weeds on their own. Their physical needs must be tended, their attitudes shaped, their habits formed, their talents trained. Because this is a male—female world (and God made it so), both male and female influences ought to go into this care and training.

And psychologically, a permanent relationship is desirable. This is a lonely world, full of possibilities for neglect and even hurt. Each of us needs someone who cares and cares deeply. Each of us needs someone who tries to understand and keeps loving us when understanding fails. Each of us needs someone with whom we can be ourselves, before whom we can be weak, against whom we can test and sharpen our deepest thoughts. Life cannot help but lack luster when this is not so. Friendship goes a long way toward meeting this need. But the best friendship of all is the permanent bond between a man and a woman who do not find "till death do us part" too long a time.

Spiritually, permanence in marriage is crucial. In a striking passage, Paul reminds his friends at Ephesus of one of the verses we are studying: *"For this reason a man shall leave his father and mother and be joined to his wife, and the two shall become one"* (Eph. 5:31). Paul goes on to make a direct connection between the marriage relationship and the bonds that tie Christ to his church: *"This is a great mystery,"* Paul acknowledges, *"and I take it to mean Christ and the church"* (Eph. 5:32).

The going may be a little rough here, but let's stick together and see what Paul means. The great marriage, the ultimate bond, the union for which the world was created, is the relationship between Christ and his church. This covenant between God and men—worked out in the life, death, and resurrection of Jesus—is what human life and human history are all about.

Marriages, then, (let's be more personal) our marriages, are supposed to be earthly, tangible, concrete, specific demonstrations of God's eternal covenant with his people. God does not quit. He sticks with his church through thick and thin, just as he clung to his people Israel in her crooked and perverse wanderings as well as in her days of righteousness and justice.

God's pledge never to leave us or forsake us is the prototype of our marriage vows. The greatest challenge we face in life is to let our lives in loyalty and love reflect God's constancy. Christ showed us the way by his own example: *"Having loved his own who were in*

29

the world, he loved them to the end" (John 13:1).

Let's waste no time arguing over the difficulties of this. If man had been able to love this way on his own he would not have needed a Savior to die for him and rise again. He would not have needed the Holy Spirit to give him power to recognize and deal with his selfishness. Sure it is hard, but it is also crucial. To fail to see this essential link between the Christian gospel and our marriages is to miss the meaning of both.

Some of you may feel that it is too late. Your marriages have utterly collapsed. Divorce has already taken place. I can only urge you to apply God's truth to your lives as faithfully as you can. Where reconciliation is still possible, work at it; where not, seek God's forgiveness for failure, and build your future life on his insights.

Some of you are ready to marry. Let the lordly love of Jesus Christ help you to stand by your commitments, to rejoice in your vows, to celebrate God's faithfulness by your fidelity.

And let those of us who are already married with some degree of satisfaction give to our marriages the time, care, love, and energy that they deserve. If marriage—permanent, binding, faithful marriage—is so important to God's program that he chose it as a way of reflecting his eternal love for his people, then how high a priority should we give to it?

PRAYER: Heavenly Father, we are frightened by our own fickleness. This makes your love all the more amazing. Give us the tenderness to be open to those who need our love, and the toughness to accept those who mistreat our love. Let us learn to love from the one who wrote love's textbook, namely Jesus Christ. His love was so loyal and so lasting that he did not shirk even a cross for the sake of his bride. In his name and strength we pray. Amen.

For further study on the permanency of marriage, refer to the following Scripture passages: Matthew 19:1–9; Mark 10:1–12; Romans 7:1–3; 1 Corinthians 7:39–40.

3

Is Marriage for Better or for Worse?

Likewise you wives, be submissive to your husbands, so that some, though they do not obey the word, may be won without a word by the behavior of their wives, when they see your reverent and chaste behavior. Let not yours be the outward adorning with braiding of hair, decoration of gold, and wearing of robes, but let it be the hidden person of the heart with the imperishable jewel of a gentle and quiet spirit, which in God's sight is very precious.

Likewise you husbands, live considerately with your wives, bestowing honor on the woman as the weaker sex, since you are joint heirs of the grace of life, in order that your prayers may not be hindered.

3

Is Marriage for Better or for Worse?

1 Peter 3:1–4, 7

"For better or for worse"—whoever put that phrase in the wedding ceremony knew what he was talking about. The ups and downs of marriage, the points of tension, the varieties of difficulties defy counting. Young people often come to the wedding day starry-eyed with idealism. Oh, they know that some couples have adjustments to make and they are partly prepared for this, but they think their special brand of intense, passionate love is going to oil the waters for smooth sailing.

Any experienced couple, however, knows that hidden rocks and contrary winds pose daily threats to domestic tranquility. As they listen to a wedding service their memories write an extended commentary or even produce a documentary film on the words "for better or for worse."

The bridal pair smile at each other in naive commitment. The veterans in the audience nod in knowing awareness. The younger couple are sure that their union will be "for better," and they voice the words "for worse" in deference to tradition. The older couple know that these words are included for more than poetic reasons. They are prepared for the "for worse" and grateful for the "for better."

What is it that makes marriage so difficult? In part, of course, it's the differences between us as partners. We live close together, bound to each other, limited by the desires, habits, schedule of our spouse. We have a good deal in common—same bed, same menu, same checkbook, same children. Yet we may be very different. Our tastes, our attitudes, our values, our dispositions were all shaped by the different roofs under which we were raised. Almost without knowing it, we have developed firm and fixed ideas about the various aspects of marriage. Male-female relationships, religious values, tidiness in the home, policies for spending and saving, personal cleanliness—these and other areas of life are trouble spots. The stronger, more rigid our convictions are, the more opportunity there is for conflict.

What makes marriages take a turn for the worse? Financial problems were the number one culprit according to a recent survey. And obviously lack of emotional and physical communication is a generous contributor to heartbreak and separation.

But at root it is our inability to accept each other as we really are that sabotages our marriages. Where criticism is a commodity and forgiveness is in short supply, you have a ready market for marital disaster.

It is just here that the Apostle Peter has a good word for us, and Peter was a married man by the way. Remember how Christ healed Peter's mother-in-law

(Mark 1:30–31), and how Paul reminded the Corinthian church that Peter took his wife with him on his preaching missions (1 Cor. 9:5). Peter reminds the husbands in the churches that looked to him for leadership that husbands and wives together *are joint heirs of the grace of life"* (1 Pet. 3:7).

How Grace Works

It's this note of grace that makes the difference. Where it's lacking, marriages cannot help but turn bad. Let's try to see how and why grace works.

It's no strain, of course, to document our need for grace. We husbands and wives push each other to measure up to our expectations. We form fantasies about what a husband or wife should be and then blame our partners for failing to fulfill them. With memories like elephants we recall past mistakes and then make damning generalities out of them. "You always do that," or "you men are all alike."

Judgment and condemnation hang heavier in many kitchens than they do in most courtrooms. And for countless couples sharp rejection of each other has become a way of life. Either they know nothing of God's grace or fail to apply it to marriage.

Sound family life must be based on the great doctrines of the Bible. Our very capacity to marry is due to God's mighty act in creation, when he made us in his image, male and female. And God has designed marriage for his purposes: to carry on the race so that there will be people who honor him as their God, to establish rich relationships that allow men and women to grow and thrive as persons, and to demonstrate his own love by giving human illustrations of it in marriage. In its intense concern and selflessness—deliberate selflessness—mature marriage is to reflect God's love. In its permanence and steadfastness marriage is to be a reminder of the everlasting covenant God has made with his people through Jesus Christ.

And this word of Peter's links marriage to the Christian gospel with its message of grace and forgiveness. To put it simply, he is saying control your attitude toward those who share your life and love with the grace that gripped your lives when God called you to be his.

A word first to the husbands because it is to them that Peter gives his reminder of grace. *"Live considerately with your wives, bestowing honor on the woman as the weaker sex, since you are joint heirs of the grace of life"* (1 Pet. 3:7). Because of the husband's position of authority and responsibility in the home, this admonition is especially fitting.

Power corrupts. And power or authority in marriage is no exception. Bossy, pushy husbands who lord it over their families and crush the spirits of their wives, who compete when they should inspire, who act tough when tenderness is called for, need to hear this note of grace.

"Joint heirs of the grace of life"—we husbands should write that on our right hands and foreheads. We too live by grace. And we must never forget it. God thinks no more of us than he does of our wives and children. His grace in Jesus Christ reaches to them and takes them as they are.

"Joint heirs of the grace of life"—this thought keeps us husbands humble. What we are and have God has given. But it also gives dignity to our wives. God has

shared his greatest gifts with them too, when they have come to know him in Jesus Christ. Abuse of women was an everyday pagan practice, and still is. It is a keen awareness of the grace of Christ that turns abuse to honor.

This grace guards us against our tendency to be irresponsible as husbands. Men tend to have shallower roots than women, drifting from place to place, leaving abandoned families behind. Appalling! impossible! we cry as we read a tragic story of a careless man who walks out on his responsibilities. But we have our own weaknesses and lapses that we ought to face—too tired at night to spend time with our youngsters, too preoccupied with our work to listen to our wives. "Don't bother me," or "you take care of that," we say.

Grace has a way of calling us to our responsibilities. God by his grace has seized our lives and commandeered them to do his will. Our new life of love has to begin with our nearest neighbors, those with whom we share roof and table, name and bed.

Peter does not forget wives and the demands God's grace puts upon them. Their lives are to be different too, transformed by the power of the gospel. Gone are the nagging and the chiding, the hostile and anxious sermonizing, replaced by a gentle and quiet spirit. Modesty and gentleness are the two virtues Peter focuses on: *"Let not yours be the outward adorning with braiding of hair, decoration of gold, and wearing of robes, but let it be the hidden person of the heart with the imperishable jewel of a gentle and quiet spirit, which in God's sight is very precious"* (1 Pet. 3:3—4).

Modesty and gentleness—Peter's choice of womanly essentials—are well taken, not so much because women want to be brazen and brash, but because we husbands often tempt them to be that way. We put so much emphasis on physical beauty—on sex appeal—that we encourage even modest women to pay undue attention to face and figure. And often we are so insensitive to their inner needs or so deaf to their intuition that we force them to needle and wheedle their way through life.

Why Grace Works

Grace corrects our perspectives. This is one reason it works so well in our lives. Grace urges us to respond at the point of the other person's deepest need. We usually expend our energies and budget our efforts for the highest possible return. Who can do me the most good? Where can I plug-in to the strongest current of influence? Grace, God's grace, tells us that ministering, not using, is the way to live.

Grace also changes our priorities. *"Bestowing honor on the woman as the weaker sex"* is one of God's requirements (1 Pet. 3:7). We give priority to the strong, the wealthy, the influential. We honor the brilliant scholar, the superb athlete, the powerful statesman. God says, "Learn from the way my grace works—honor the weak." We place priority on physical beauty—flowing hair, a flawless face, a shapely form. God says, "Put your emphasis on the inner person, the real self, made in my image and therefore of inestimable value. That's what *my* grace does."

Grace works in our lives, and especially in our married lives, because it links us to God's purposes. It was to show his grace and reveal his glory that God created us in the first place. And he sent his Son to make this grace and glory unmistakably clear. *"We beheld his glory . . . full of grace and truth"* (John 1:14). To live graciously is to live as Christ lived; to live graciously is to show that the gospel of God's grace is power not just words.

Marriage can be for better, but only when husband and wife are really *"joint heirs of the grace of life"* and treat each other as such. Let the grace that changed your relationship to God change your relationship to each other. This grace is available in ample supply. For your marriage and your life there is nothing in the world better than that.

PRAYER: God of all grace, teach us how to live on your terms. Help us as husbands to view our wives as honored, esteemed partners in your love. Help our wives to nurture their inward beauty. Show us the intimate connection between our spiritual lives and our marital responsibilities, and forgive us for fencing life into compartments. You have told us that effective prayer and faithful witness are dependent on how we treat each other. This scares us, but in our fear we want to seek fresh grace. We know your supply of grace never runs out because we have seen Jesus Christ who is full of grace. In his name we take courage to pray. Amen.

For further study of related themes, refer to the following passages: Matthew 18:21–22; Mark 11:25 26; Luke 6:37; 2 Corinthians 2:10; 1 Peter 4:10.

THE GUIDELINES
IN THE FAMILY

4

Does Father Know Best?

Be subject to one another out of reverence for Christ. Wives, be subject to your husbands, as to the Lord. For the husband is the head of the wife as Christ is the head of the church, his body, and is himself its Savior. As the church is subject to Christ, so let wives also be subject in everything to their husbands.

4

Does Father Know Best?

Ephesians 5:21–24

Marriage is a delicate system of checks and balances. And I don't mean the checks with which we pay our bills or the balances we struggle to maintain in our bank accounts. For most of us that's a delicate system too.

The checks and balances of marriage are like those of government. Responsibilities are divided and different roles assigned to each branch. Congress passes laws which the executive branch, headed by the president, enforces, while the supreme court judges whether or not the laws are in harmony with the constitution.

So in marriage husband, wife, and children all have their special responsibilities and make their unique contributions within the family. The Apostle Paul was evidently a bachelor, but he knew the importance of family life. In at least two of his letters (Ephesians and Colossians) he gave clear instructions to all three branches of the family—husbands, wives, children. Like a triangle the family must have these three sides to be complete. And like a three-legged stool each member of

47

the family must fulfill his or her responsibilities if the family is to be steady and stable.

Paul's counsel to the family is plain and to the point: *"Wives, be subject to your husbands as to the Lord ... Husbands, love your wives, as Christ loved the church ... Children, obey your parents in the Lord, for this is right ... Fathers, do not provoke your children to anger, but bring them up in the discipline and instruction of the Lord"* (Eph. 5:22, 25; 6:1, 4).

The apostle did not leave Christian family structure and relationships to chance. Nor did he advise different patterns for different cultures. His concerns were not primarily sociological but theological. It was not custom or taste but biblical teaching that determined how our families should be ordered.

We have seen that our marriages and our family life have profound spiritual significance. Marriage is not just a convenient, comfortable way for two people to live together and take care of each other's physical and emotional needs. It is not just a way of pooling skills so that a husband can have hot meals, clean sheets, and mended socks in exchange for the food and shelter he provides his wife.

Our marriages were designed for higher purposes like expressing God's love and illustrating the covenant, the enduring pledge, he has given to his people. Marriage was designed by God to help us be full and whole persons—sharing, loving, caring, providing. Life was not meant to be lived in lonely isolation but in rich and gracious fellowship. Whole men and women are what God wanted when he made us in his image, male and female. And mature, devout, godly marriage makes a key contribution to this wholeness.

Our marriages should be tied to the Christian gospel as well as to God's creation and his covenant. God's creation with all its beauty and power and God's covenant with all of its love and wonder are acts of God's grace. He created because he wanted to—not because he had to. He called us to be his people not because we deserved it but because he desired us. And husband and wife alike share that legacy of grace if they have looked to Christ as the answer to life's problems. The good news of the Christian gospel has no labels on it to restrict its circulation. It is not for the wealthy only, the experienced only, the learned only, or for men only. It knows no boundaries of race, station, or sex: *"There is neither Jew nor Greek, there is neither slave nor free, there is neither male nor female; for you are all one in Christ Jesus"* (Gal. 3:28).

The Husband's Role

This gospel which lays hold of our lives and draws us to Christ also changes every area of our living—especially our family life. Every member of the family is affected in this application of the gospel. What Paul wrote to his friends at Ephesus and Colosse was not just sage advice for peaceful living. It was Christian doctrine, based on who we are as God's people and what Jesus has done for us.

Take, for instance, his instruction to the wives: *"Wives, be subject to your husbands, as to the Lord. For the husband is the head of the wife as Christ is the head of the church, his body, and is himself its*

49

Savior. As the church is subject to Christ, so let wives also be subject in everything to their husbands" (Eph. 5:22—24).

This is not just strategy that Paul i s recommending. He is not encouraging wives to respond to their husbands' leading as a tactic to get their own way. His advice is practical to be sure, but it is practical not just because it works but because it is grounded on biblical truth; and biblical truth is always practical. It was meant to be applied.

The husband is to be the leader in the home as Christ is the leader of his church. Note that I said leader not boss. To understand Christ's leadership which blazes the trail for ours we have to look at two scenes in his ministry.

Scene 1 took place on his final journey to Jerusalem, the journey that led to the cross (Mark 10:32—45). James and John had heard Jesus talk about power and glory, and they were hungry for a taste of them. *"Grant us to sit, one at your right hand and one at your left, in your glory"* (Mark 10:37). Jesus told them in no uncertain terms that appointments to positions of power and authority were under God's jurisdiction. Then he seized the moment to teach some basic lessons about Christian leadership. *"You know that those who are supposed to rule over the Gentiles lord it over them, and their great men exercise authority over them. But it shall not be so among you; but whoever would be great among you must be your servant, and whoever would be first among you must be slave of all. For the Son of man also came not to be served but to serve, and to give his life as a ransom for many"* (Mark 10:42—45). We husbands can well begin to squirm when we compare that style—that servant style—of leadership with our own.

Scene 2 is set in the room where Jesus met with his disciples just before his arrest and trial. The Master was fully aware of what was going to happen to him and what his death would mean to the whole world. And he *"rose from supper, laid aside his garments, and girded himself with a towel. Then he poured water into a basin, and began to wash the disciples' feet, and to wipe them with the towel with which he was girded"* (John 13:4—5). At his high moment of glory, Jesus, the leader and husband of his church, practiced what he had preached. He became a servant.

As servant-leader, leader-servant of the family, the husband is to be the provider for the basic needs of the household. And more than material provision is needed though that is certainly part of his responsibility.

He must provide authority. The security of wife and children is directly dependent on the husband's ability to determine what is best for his family and then to see that it is done. Patience to work on a problem, wisdom to see the best solution, and courage to carry it out are what we as husbands ought to seek from God. Sin is always at work in our kind of world, and it does not stop at the front door of our homes. Willful wives and stubborn children are more the rule than the exception. And father himself is no paragon of virtue. He, too, stands in need of great forgiveness. He may not always know best, but he is always father and must seek to do his best for the sake of his family who need the firm and tender discipline that he alone can bring.

He must provide guidance. The spiritual and intellectual nurture of his wife and children are his responsibility. Their understanding of what life is all about, their ability to cope with temptation, their education in the Christian faith—in all of these the father's influence is crucial. "Like father, like son" was never truer than in these areas. Our twigs are apt to take on our crookedness and become bent, contorted trees. What we as husbands are is at least as important as what we do.

The Husband's Responsibility

Leader? Yes! Boss? No! This is made startlingly clear with the command: *"Husbands, love your wives, as Christ loved the church and gave himself up for her"* (Eph. 5:25). This is the most awesome responsibility of all. Our financial obligations and our job commitments pale into insignificance beside this. I as a husband am to love my wife with the kind of loyalty and selflessness that Christ demonstrated to his church. *"But God shows his love for us in that while we were yet sinners Christ died for us"* (Rom. 5:8).

Of the husband alone is this love required. *"Be subject"* is the verb prescribed for our wives. And *"honor"* is the requirement of our children. But *"love," "love as Christ loved,"* is the burden imposed upon us as husbands. This keeps our authority from degenerating into brutal power. This makes faithful, responsible servants out of us rather than ruthless bosses.

Father may not know best. In fact he may have a lot to learn. But God the loving and wise Father has placed him as leader and has called him to love. This is a difficult role and an awesome responsibility, but the heavenly Father who really does know best offers his example and his power to all of us earthly fathers who want so desperately to know and to do what is best.

And the rest of the family can help us. Wives and children, unless your Christian conscience says no, your privilege is to follow the leadership of your husband and father. God will hold him responsible for wise and loving decisions. He will hold you responsible for loyal support and gracious obedience. Father may not always know best, but with God's help and your encouragement he'll be right most of the time. And God's grace will take care of the rest.

PRAYER: Heavenly Father, none of us as husbands can stand before your Word and claim obedience. Forgive our foolish attempts to use our power for our gain. Forgive our lack of sensitivity to the deep needs of those who depend on us for provision, authority, guidance. Let your love become our largest aim. Hear, too, our wives and children as they seek to put your gospel at the center of their home life. Bind our families together with the uncuttable cords of love and loyalty. Engrave the towel and basin on each family's coat of arms that graceful service to each other may be our most familiar trait. These things we pray in the name of One who nourishes and cherishes us as members of his church. Amen.

For further study of related themes, refer to the following passages: Matthew 15:1—6; 1 Corinthians 11:3; Colossians 3:16—24.

5

Is Mother's Place in the Home?

Husbands, love your wives, as Christ loved the church and gave himself up for her, that he might sanctify her, having cleansed her by the washing of water with the word, that he might present the church himself in splendor, without spot or wrinkle or any such thing, that she might be holy and without blemish. Even so husbands should love their wives as their own bodies. He who loves his wife loves himself.

5

Is Mother's Place in the Home?

Ephesians 5:25–28

A young mother wearing a track suit? That's the way a current television commercial acknowledges that a mother's life is lived on the run. With the steady pace of a long distance runner she keeps at her work from early morning till late at night.

Her work is varied as well as constant. If she wore a different uniform for each of her tasks, she would have a closet full of them and change twenty times a day. Cook, housekeeper, laundress, business manager, nurse, teacher, chauffeur, coach, counselor, gardener, lover—these and other vocations all fall within her range of responsibilities.

It has always been so. Modern life in some ways may have increased the pace, but it has not changed the basic demands that caring for a husband and family make on a mother's time and energy. The Book of Proverbs contains a remarkable description of the way a good wife carries on her work. Listen to the amazing combination of skills that she possesses:

> *"She seeks wool and flax,*
> *and works with willing hands.*
> *She is like the ships of the merchant,*
> *she brings her food from afar.*

57

She rises while it is yet night
and provides food for her household
and tasks for her maidens.
She considers a field and buys it;
with the fruit of her hand she plants a vineyard"
(Prov. 31:13–16).

And her industry is matched by her compassion:

"She opens her hands to the poor,
and reaches out her hands to the needy.
She opens her mouth with wisdom,
and the teaching of kindness is on her tongue"
(Prov. 31:20, 26).

No wonder she has her children's blessing and her husband's praise. And so did many other wives in the Bible. Biblical faith has affirmed the beauty, wonder, and dignity of being a woman. It has also protected the rights of women in a time and culture that often treated them shabbily. The Ten Commandments, for instance, make no distinction between the parents—both mother and father are to be honored. Adultery is outlawed, and even coveting a neighbor's wife is forbidden (Exod. 20:12, 14, 17).

The Bible makes it clear from cover to cover that women are to be treated as persons not as property. And its portraits of illustrious women underscore this. For Hannah, the biblical writer had unbridled admiration as she poured out her devotion to God, trusting him for a son and then giving that son, Samuel, back to God to serve him as priest and prophet. And Esther's courage before her king in a time of danger to her people ranks her in the highest echelon of history's great women. Then, too, there's the unnamed woman in the Song of Solomon. Her passionate ardor for her lover and her delightful response to his wooing show that a good wife does a lot more for a husband than cooking his breakfast and ironing his shirts.

The Old Testament celebrates womanhood in a host of ways. But the New Testament adds even greater honor and dignity to the role of a wife. It spends little time detailing her duties but puts great emphasis on her relationship to her husband. The key passage is Ephesians 5:24: *"As the church is subject to Christ, so let wives also be subject in everything to their husbands."* After showing how the wife is like the church and how the husband is to demonstrate Christ's love, Paul summarizes his thought: *"However, let each one of you love his wife as himself, and let the wife see that she respects her husband"* (Eph. 5:33).

What "Be Subject" Does Not Mean

It's easy for us to misinterpret the words *be subject*. It should not mean a loss of the wife's identity. She is not to be crushed by her husband or absorbed by her children. God made her what she is with her special set of gifts and talents. These she is to cultivate for God's glory and service.

Your individuality is God-given. Treat it as such. Housework with its dull routines and endless cycle of chores need not be a threat to individuality if you see it as an opportunity to show your love for family and your devotion to God. Be yourself, add your own

59

touches to what you do. God made you to be yourself with all your strengths. Use them to the full for your family and for him.

For a wife to be subject to her husband does not mean a compromise of the wife's conscience. In our sinfulness we as husbands may ask our wives to do just that. And in your sinfulness you as wives may be tempted to give in and avoid a struggle. When your conscience is involved, stick to your convictions, but be sure your conscience is taking its orders from the Bible as God's own Word and not from your whims, hunches, or intuition. Your husband is not your god; both you and he need to remember that. He does not have sovereignty over you—body, soul, and spirit—but he is your leader, commissioned by God to give support and direction, guidance and instruction to the entire family.

Being subject to her husband does not reduce a wife to slavery. Of course, she is to don the garb of servant, but so are all Christians. Young and old, rich and poor, male and female—all are free in Christ and all are slaves whose highest joy is serving others. The Christian husband leads the family in straight paths only when he leads them as their servant. Husbands and wives together are servants of the greater Master. They do not boss each other. They seek to serve each other as *"joint heirs of the grace of life"* (1 Pet. 3:7)

What "Be Subject" Does Mean

No loss of identity, no compromise of conscience, no reduction to slavery—this is clear. There is no relationship ordained by God which should reduce us to being less than persons. What then does Paul mean when he says, *"so let wives also be subject in everything to their husbands"* (Eph. 5:24)?

For one thing, he means that she supports her husband's authority before their children. A divided family is as unstable as the double-minded man that James warns against (James 1:7—8). Children want to respect their parents, and yet they constantly test us to see if we are worthy of that respect. If we undercut each other and allow our children to divide us or to play one against the other, we give our youngsters what they really dread.

True, sometimes our wives have better judgment than we husbands. They can well begin to fidgit and squirm when we make plans that go against their grain. We ought to encourage our wives and children to help us make decisions which affect them. At the same time, the final responsibility is the husband's and he must do what seems best. Unless it's a matter of Christian conscience, the wife should back her husband all the way. If he's wrong, chances are that he'll learn from the bad experience and do better next time. And his plan may work out better than the wife thinks it will. After all, as a good friend once taught me, there are usually a lot of ways to do the right thing.

Better to settle for second best and retain family unity than for the wife to divide the family, erode her husband's confidence, and attack her children's sense of security by degrading their daddy before their eyes.

For a wife to be subject to her husband also means that she accepts her role as wife and does what only she can do. God made us male and female in the beginning. Yet when sin entered human experience the first act of the man and woman was to doubt the rightness of their masculinity and femininity. The fig leaves with which they covered themselves are a terrible reminder of our failure to know what God expected of us when he made us as men and women. One of the great gifts a Christian husband and wife can give each other is reassurance about who they are as man and woman. Neither need compete with the other. And neither is complete, physically, emotionally, intellectually without the other. The wife, by her gentleness, can add to her husband's strength and mellow it at the same time. She can respect his wisdom and insights and enrich them by her intuition. Her wifely support and loyalty will be used by God's grace to cause her husband to thrive.

This kind of subjection, finally, means that the wife demonstrates the church's response to Christ. The first clause is crucial: *"As the church is subject to Christ"* (Eph. 5:24). We are not left to write our own rules for marriage or to develop our own job descriptions. The highest purpose of marriage is to express in kitchen and bedroom, in community club and shopping center, in office and factory the great secret of all life—that God through Jesus is forming a people to love and serve him. These people support Christ's authority and offer him full obedience in response to his amazing and costly love.

The drabness would drop from our marriages and the problems that loom large would shrink into perspective. if we could once get this into our hearts and minds. Then we could begin to fathom what a mother's place in the home really is.

Home, of course, is people more than place. Some mothers can't stay home all the time. Their circumstances and abilities insist that they work outside the home. But their work should have the home as its purpose and the family's welfare as its aim. As the church's chief role is to carry out Christ's work in our world, so the Christian wife and mother has the high duty of serving her husband and children in the name of Christ.

This kind of loyal service is never easy. Sin is at work in all our lives to make loving terribly difficult. But the great Husband of the church who loved his Bride so much that he gave his life for her stands ready to help with all the resources of heaven at his disposal. What goes on in your living room and kitchen and bedroom is of incalculable importance to him. Whether you work within the home or outside it is not the key issue. What really counts is whether you are letting Christ make you all you can be to those for whom your love and loyalty are indispensable.

PRAYER: Lord of our hearts and homes, we need your help. Many of us wives and husbands have found that marriage is a rocky road. If we knew more about your love we would be better able to find our way through the rough places and around the turns. Teach us why marriage is important to you so that we will know why it should be important to us. It's not so much advice that we want—we're swamped with that. But it's the power to be to each other what the other needs. We believe that Christ is our answer. Now help our unbelief. In his strong name, we pray. Amen.

For further study of related themes, refer to the following passages: Psalm 113:9; 1 Timothy 2:10–15; Titus 2:4–5.

6

Can We Treat Children like People?

Children, obey your parents in the Lord, for this is right. "Honor your father and mother" (this is the first commandment with a promise), "that it may be well with you and that you may live long on the earth." Fathers do not provoke your children to anger, but bring them up in the discipline and instruction of the Lord.

6

Can We Treat Children like People?

Ephesians 6:1–4

For most of us extremes come easy. It's balance that's hard to come by. Overreaction is almost a way of life with us. Our basic posture is not standing up straight but bending over backwards. We don't move freely; we ricochet our way through life.

This tendency toward extremism is especially pronounced in the way we raise our children. In discipline, for instance, steadiness and consistency are virtues rarely found. We volley back and forth between strict regulation and open permissiveness, with a good deal of nagging and chiding in between.

In turn we may neglect and then spoil our youngsters. Victims of our guilt feelings we overcompensate when we feel we've done the wrong thing. Or we try to give our children what we never had. In sparing them the deprivations of our youth we sometimes deprive them of experiences that help them grow. After all, learning to cope with frustration bravely, to take disappointment cheerfully, to do without gracefully is part of growing up. This younger generation of ours is physically larger and healthier than almost any in history. But those of us who raised them may have overprotected them, with the result that they may lack the toughness and discipline that come from hardship.

In other cases, our youngsters have felt unimportant, even unwanted. They've had to take second place to our other aspirations. Our deep drives to succeed in business were sharpened by the great depression. And we'll knock ourselves out to ward off the poverty which burned us so deeply as children. Consequently, we have been willing to risk personal health and family stability in order to gain financial security.

Or social aspirations may have caused us to push our families into the background. The desire to be known in the right circles, to belong to the best clubs, to be recognized in the community has lured a lot of us to spend our spare time away from home.

And don't forget how confused we've been about our authority over our children. We often fuss and fume at them over trivials. They become pincushions for our own anxieties and insecurities as we jab and needle them over things that have no consequence. At the same time we may turn lax and fearful when their real welfare is at stake. The permissiveness of our age is monumental. We want so badly to be pals with our children that we end up not being parents. Pals they can have many; parents, only two. If the two shirk their responsibilities and fail to give the proper support in love, authority, and discipline, the youngsters are at a loss as to how to grow up. Other influences fill the authority vacuum, and mutiny or desertion is the result.

Balance is our problem. How do we treat children like people—people made by God and committed to us to be prepared for fine and full living? The Bible has not abandoned us here any more than it has in the other aspects of family life. The great doctrines of the faith—our creation in God's image, our covenant relationship with him through Christ, our freedom in the gospel to be forgiven and to forgive—all have things to say to children and parents.

Not that the Bible tells us what to do in every situation. It is not a handbook on children. It is the textbook of salvation. But our Christian families are part of God's program of salvation. Parents who raise children to know and fear God's name play a key role in what God is doing in the world. And children who honor their parents are object lessons to friends and neighbors of the reverence and respect we owe to God, who is the Father of us all.

Not so much specific words of advice for every problem but principles that we can apply to the changing needs of life—these are what the Bible gives. Paul's words in Ephesians 6 are especially helpful as we seek to avoid the extremes to which we're so prone. They deal with the ties between children and parents in a context which outlines the responsibilities of each member of the family. This in itself is a reminder of the importance of children. They too are people, bound together with us in the network of life, intimately tied to God's plan to rescue a people who will make true worship their highest aim.

Children Are to Be Treated with Dignity

"Children, obey your parents in the Lord, for this is right. 'Honor your father and mother' . . . (Eph. 6:1–2). Paul reaches into the heart of the Ten Commandments

for these words which show how important the parent-child relationship is to God.

Though the commandment is given to children the parent's responsibilities are implicit in it. Our first responsibility is to remember that our children belong more to God than to us. This means they are to be treated with dignity. He has high hopes and fine plans for them, and he counts on us to help them be what he wants them to be.

We don't own our children. We have them as a trust from God who commissions us to lead them in paths of righteousness for his name's sake. Jesus reminded his disciples that our loyalty to him takes priority even over our loyalty to our parents: *"If any one comes to me and does not hate his own father and mother and wife and children and brothers and sisters, yes, and even his own life, he cannot be my disciple"* (Luke 14:26). Strong language this. The same God who commanded us to honor our parents here insists that we hate them for his sake. What Jesus means, of course, in this Hebrew type of overstatement is that we are to put him first. Our relationship with him outranks everything else.

As we teach our children the dignity of being human, we teach them to honor God even above us, their parents. We do this best by the way we honor God. Our second responsibility in helping our children obey God's command is to be sure that we honor our children as persons made for God. Where do children learn what honor and obedience mean? From our example. Our respect for them is the best way to insure their regard for us. Some people think children are to be broken like wild horses. But our ultimate aim is to relate to our children not to ride them. It is their maturity not our mastery that we must seek. We may browbeat them to respond to us, but we should rear them to cope with themselves and the rest of life.

Our third responsibility is to remind our children that honoring others adds to our own dignity as persons. This is particularly true of our attitude toward parents. We are so much a part of our parents—their fingerprints are all over us—that what they are cannot be separated from what we have become. Any person who detracts from his parents' dignity—whatever their station in life or however they have treated him—diminishes his own sense of worth. To put it simply, hurting others always hurts us more. And the closer the other person, the deeper the hurt.

Children Are to Be Prepared for Responsibility

Can we treat children like people? Sure we can, by treating them with dignity and preparing them for responsibility. Again the checks and balances that Paul uses come into play. The wife is to respect her husband as the church does Christ. The husband is to love the wife as Christ loves the church. Each has privileges, and each has responsibilities. Similarly, while children are called to obey their parents, the parents are commanded not to *"provoke your children to anger, but bring them up in the discipline and instruction of the Lord"* (Eph. 6:4). Always a realist, Paul knows that we parents are as much flawed by sin as our children are. We can easily pervert the commandment that calls for their obedience into a personal power play. Paul's warning is wholesome: our task is not to lord it over our youngsters but to prepare them for their own Christian service.

"The discipline and instruction of the Lord"—this is not just factual information about the Bible. It is thorough, consistent training in what it means to be a Christian. There is no way to delegate this training to Sunday school classes or young people's meetings, though they may have a share. The basic responsibility rests with us as parents.

"The discipline and instruction of the Lord"—our equipment to be responsible Christians and wholesome human beings. To bank on the love of Christ is the first thing we ought to teach our young people about the Christian faith. Our first thoughts ought not to be of our duty but of Christ's love. A good thing it is for us to teach our children to sing "Jesus loves me, this I know, for the Bible tells me so." God's love for us is the prime truth of the universe, the best news to be found in heaven or on earth. Let's make it so clear in our teaching and living that our children will feel it in their bones even before they understand it with their minds.

To follow Christ's ways is the second great lesson we must both learn and teach if we are to treat our children like people—preparing them to assume responsibility. To follow Christ is to say yes to God's love by loving him and sharing his love with others. Again, our emphasis should not be primarily on the law with its demands but on God's grace which sets us free to follow Christ, as we learn his values and draw our strength from him.

Dignity and responsibility have been at the center of our thinking because they are the mix of our manhood.

No one who is robbed of his dignity or who shirks his responsibility can truly be a person. The relationship between parent and child with its mutual delights and obligations is God's way of affirming our dignity and preparing us for responsibility.

More than that, our relationships with each other teach us lessons about our relationships with God. In total concern for our children's welfare, we parents get a glimpse into the depths of God's grace. And in our wholesome balance of authority and compassion our children sense something of the fatherhood of God. How good of God to put us in families! Let's make the most of this special act of his goodness.

PRAYER: Our Heavenly Father, people you have made us, and people you want us to be. Forgive our desire to play God for others, even for our children. And forgive us our temptation to use them as pawns for our success or toys for our pleasure. You made them and us for better things—your worship and service. Give us power to seek those better things for your name's sake. Amen.

For further study of related themes, refer to the following passages: Psalm 131; Proverbs 10:1, 15:20; Matthew 18:1–6; Mark 10:13–16; Luke 18:15–17.

THE MINISTRY
OF THE FAMILY

7

How's Your Weekday Worship?

"Now therefore fear the Lord, and serve him in sincerity and in faithfulness; put away the gods which your fathers served beyond the River, and in Egypt, and serve the Lord. And if you be unwilling to serve the Lord, choose this day whom you will serve, whether the gods your fathers served in the region beyond the River, or the gods of the Amorites in whose land you dwell; but as for me and my house, we will serve the Lord."

7

How's Your Weekday Worship?

Joshua 24:14-15

What makes man man? That's not an easy question to answer. We have so much in common with other members of the animal kingdom that it's hard to put a finger on our uniqueness. We have to build machines to help us do what birds and fish do naturally.

Man works and works well, but so do ants, bees, and beavers. With a discipline and industry that leave most of us breathless, these creatures tackle colossal projects and carry them off with a flourish. Solomon and the other wise men of Israel knew that in many areas men could learn profitable lessons from the animal kingdom. *"Go to the ant, O sluggard; consider her ways, and be wise. Without having any chief, officer or ruler, she prepares her food in summer, and gathers her sustenance in harvest"* (Prov. 6:6-8). The wise men not only learned from the patterns of the animals but were baffled by their prowess: *"Three things are too wonderful for me; four I do not understand: the way of an eagle in the sky, the way of a serpent on a rock, the way of a ship on the high seas, and the way of a man with a maiden"* (Prov. 30:18–19).

Man speaks and speaks clearly. Surely this capacity to phrase his thoughts in language, to make his needs and feelings known in words is what makes man man. We can scarcely dispute the importance of man's use of verbal symbols. But animals too have their ways of communicating. Let one or two ants discover an open jam jar or a slice of spiced luncheon meat and before long the whole ant neighborhood has heard the news and begun the march to the picnic. And much research is under way to check the means of communication among the higher mammals—especially whales, porpoises, and dolphins. We may be in for some surprises when we know the whole story about animal talk.

Man works. Man speaks. And man worships. More than anything else this makes him man. Of all God's creation, he alone is made in God's image, capable of conversing with God, enough like God to have personal fellowship with him.

Man is never more man than when he worships the God who made him. Man is always something less than man when he worships anything else. Jesus, in his conversation with the woman of Samaria, called attention to the contrast between true and false worship: *"You worship what you do not know; we worship what we know, for salvation is from the Jews. But the hour is coming, and now is, when the true worshipers will worship the Father in spirit and truth, for such the Father seeks to worship him. God is spirit, and those who worship him must worship in spirit and truth"* (John 4:22–24).

At the heart of our manhood, then, lies worship.

Since this is true, worship is utterly central to family life. One of the chief duties of the family is to help each of us to be fully human. The home is the center of worship, of fellowship, of service, and of education. There is no whole humanity, no full-blown existence, without these ingredients—worship, fellowship, service, education.

How's your weekday worship? Not that Sunday worship is unimportant. It is vital to our Christian lives that we gather week by week with God's people to celebrate Christ's resurrection and the coming of God's Spirit to the church at Pentecost. Both of these events took place on Sunday. That's why it has replaced the Sabbath as the day of rest and worship for most Christians.

A Deliberate Choice

But worship cannot be confined to weekly church services. It must be nurtured and encouraged daily within our homes. Joshua saw this clearly at the dawn of Israel's history. When the men of Israel had conquered the land of Canaan and were about to settle in the portions assigned to them, Joshua reminded them that they had a choice as to whom they would worship: *"Now therefore fear the Lord, and serve him in sincerity and in faithfulness; put away the gods which your fathers served beyond the River, and in Egypt, and serve the Lord. And if you be unwilling to serve the Lord, choose this day whom you will serve, whether the gods your fathers served in the region beyond the River, or the gods of the Amorites in whose land you dwell"* (Josh. 24:14–15).

Leader that he was, Joshua saw the issues clearly. He realized that our choice of whom to worship is a deliberate not casual choice. Idolatry is the normal way of life. No one in this troubled, rebellious world of ours just drifts into a firm relationship with the true God. The tides all run the other way. False worship comes naturally; true worship needs deliberate decision.

Urgency is the crying need as we face this decision. The issue of whom we worship, whom we choose to be our God, is the most pressing question in life, literally a matter of life and death. Some questions we can ponder awhile and decide at our leisure. Not this one. Too much is at stake. We can never know who God is or who we really are until this question is settled. That's why Joshua said, *"Choose this day whom you will serve."* No man can live an utterly godless life. He will serve some god whether he knows it or not. Life and his very nature as a creature made to worship push him to decision.

What Joshua preached he practiced: *"but as for me and my house, we will serve the Lord"* (Josh. 24:15). No waiting to see what his friends would do, no hesitating until he was sure he was in the majority, no postponing his decision until he had more evidence, Joshua made his choice with all the urgency that this ultimate, absolute, final choice demands.

The whole family is affected by this decision. Joshua speaks for himself and his family. He believes firmly that it is his responsibility as father to exercise spiritual authority over his family. Not that his faith makes theirs unnecessary, but that his leadership can provide direction for all of them. Faith is a personal matter, no doubt about it. Joshua says *"as for me."* He makes a deliberate, personal choice. Yet faith is also a family matter. We are concerned for the health and safety of our children and carefully supervise their diet and recreation. Can we be any less concerned for their worship? Our deliberate choice of the living God will give them encouragement and support to choose him too.

A Decisive Choice

When we with our families choose to serve God, his power becomes effective in our lives. Joshua's words of exhortation to his fellow Israelites at Shechem are charged with reminders of God's power. The plagues of Egypt, the rescue from the Red Sea, the conquest of Canaan—these events are paraded before the eyes of the people to jog their memories about the greatness of God's power. What other god can match these claims? The gods of Egypt? Of Canaan? Not at all! They had already been challenged by the God of Israel and roundly whipped. The power of God was unquestioned. The Israelites acknowledged this: *"For it is the Lord our God who brought us and our fathers up from the land of Egypt . . . and who did those great signs in our sight, and preserved us in all the way that we went, and among all the people through whom we passed"* (Josh. 24:17).

If these men of old felt that way about God's power, how should we feel now that Christ has risen from the dead? To choose God and to worship him means that our lives are linked to the God who works wonders, who helps us endure suffering, who steadies us

83

in persecution. The Exodus and the resurrection are his impeccable credentials.

Our choice to worship God with our families is a decisive choice because it ties us to God's power. It is decisive also because our destinies are determined by it. *"If you forsake the Lord and serve foreign gods, then he will turn and do you harm, and consume you, after having done you good"* (Josh. 24:20). Joshua's stern warning pinpoints the difference between judgment and grace. Trust God, and know his forgiveness and power. Reject him, and meet the sting of his wrath. A decisive choice indeed.

Now when you and your family have decided to make your home a center of worship, when you've followed Joshua's lead and pledge to serve the Lord, what practical steps should your family take? First, you can engage in family prayer and Bible reading. Mealtimes especially can become high moments of devotion to God. As you thank God for your food, you can lead your whole family in the constant recognition that all you have comes as a gift from God's hand. As you chat about the day's activities you can look for ways to thank God for who he is and what he has done. A few verses read or recited daily will remind your family that we live not by bread alone but by every word that comes from the mouth of God.

Another thing you can do to strengthen your weekday worship is to support the ministry of your local church. Look for ways to enjoy the blessings of Sunday throughout the week. Discuss the sermon, not critically but appreciatively. Come back to it from time to time as occasion arises. Take an interest in what your youngsters are studying in Sunday school and help them apply what they learn in their daily living.

Most of all encourage openness to God in every area of life. Learn to thank the Lord in all circumstances. My mother set a good example for me in this. Once I used a "plumber's friend" to unstop our clogged sink. When the water once more swirled down the drain, my mother said, "Thank the Lord." I thought that was strange because I had unstopped the sink. But I've learned better since. *"Give thanks in all circumstances; for this is the will of God in Christ Jesus for you"* (1 Thess. 5:18). To see God's hand in things great and small, to acknowledge his help in our accomplishments, to praise his name when things go against us—this is the stuff of worship.

More important than what we do in worship is the attitude of our hearts. When we can take it on the chin and thank God, when we can face our failures without despair and our successes without pride, when we lavish compassion on those who need it without requiring pity when our wounds ache, when we make God's will our highest aim, then our family will know what true worship—worship in spirit and in truth—is all about. And when they do, they will have discovered what it really means to be human.

PRAYER: Heavenly Father, accept our frail beginnings at worship. Idols are never far from us. Strange gods—lust, pleasure, achievement, success—court us from every side. Let your love set us straight. Let your power overwhelm us. Teach us to choose you over all competitors. Then help us to nurture our families in the deep meanings of that choice. Through Jesus Christ we pray. Amen.

For further study on the importance of your weekday worship, refer to the following Scripture passages: 1 Chronicles 16:28—34; Psalm 95:6—7; Psalm 99:5,9; Matthew 4:10.

8

Can Families Be Friends?

Behold, how good and pleasant it is
    when brothers dwell in unity!
It is like the precious oil upon the head,
    running down upon the beard,
upon the beard of Aaron,
    running down on the collar of his robes!
It is like the dew of Hermon,
    which falls on the mountains of Zion!
For there the Lord has commanded the blessing,
    life for evermore.

8

Can Families Be Friends?

Psalm 133

"Dear Abby: This is my problem . . ." "Dear Ann Landers: You won't believe the situation that exists in my family . . ." A couple of thousand letters like these appear in our newspapers over the course of a year.

Their subjects run the gamut of human problems from whom to invite to a wedding to how to deal with nosey neighbors. But day after day, year after year, one theme dominates these pleas for help—tensions within the family.

A teenage girl writes to protest her mother's practice of snooping in her diary. A frustrated bride complains because her husband is still tied to his mother's apron strings. A stepson worries that he is being treated shabbily by a parent that doesn't quite accept him. An older brother is vexed at the preferential treatment given his younger sister. And on and on.

It would be just a dreary catalog of problems if there

were not human beings attached to each. But each episode borders on tragedy, and many are well across the line.

The pain is compounded because the hurt is caused by loved ones, relatives, those who share home, name, and blood. The tragedy is heightened when those who should be allies become enemies, and the place that should be a fortress of security is turned into a bloody battle ground. No wonder we sometimes ask the question, "Can families be friends?"

This is no new question, by the way. Our warm feelings about what families used to be are usually based on our distance from the actual situations. What makes the good old days so good is that they are far enough removed so that we cannot take a close look at them.

No, family strife is part of human life this side of Adam's great rebellion. Just browse through the Bible and you'll see what I mean. Cain becomes his brother's killer instead of his keeper (Gen. 4:8–9). Jacob cheats his older brother Esau of the wealth and blessing to which his seniority entitles him (Gen. 25:29–34; 27:1–41). And this same Jacob wrongly played favorites with Joseph to the hurt of his other sons. They, in turn, wrongly gained vengeance on their father and his favorite son by contriving to have Joseph sold into slavery (Gen. 37:1–3). They even tricked their father into believing that Joseph was dead, slaughtered by a wild beast.

Family rivalry reared its ugly head in a high moment of Israel's history, just after God had rescued his people from slavery in Egypt and given them his law at Sinai. Moses is the victim this time: *"Miriam and Aaron spoke against Moses because of the Cushite woman whom he had married"* (Num. 12:1). Their petty jealousy toward their brother roused the wrath of God, and judgment, in the form of leprosy, was their lot.

Then there is the vicious story of lust and brutality in David's family. Amnon, David's son, first tried to seduce and then ravaged his sister Tamar. Absalom, another son, gained vengeance on Amnon by having him murdered while Amnon was in a drunken stupor (2 Sam. 13:1–29).

Not pretty stories these, but true. They form the background for a psalm that ought to get more attention than it does—Psalm 133: *"Behold, how good and pleasant it is when brothers dwell in unity!"* The unity of the family is important enough (and rare enough) that an entire psalm is written to celebrate it.

This is good evidence of the importance of the family in God's program to change men and women from rebels to worshipers. The home was meant to be a center of worship, worship that in no way can be confined to Sunday or to church. Together in prayer and thanksgiving the members of every family are to acknowledge daily their dependence on God. "All things bright and beautiful" are gifts of his love, without which life is impossible. The home is to be a center of service, a base for acts of charity and kindness, a place where love for neighbor becomes a way of life. Education, too, centers in the home, despite our elaborate and important systems of public and private education. The basic lessons of life, like who I am, who God is and what he has done for me, are to be learned in the home. So are the values and standards that shape us as responsible men and women.

The Power of Fellowship

The home is a center of fellowship. *"How good and pleasant it is when brothers dwell in unity!"* The psalmist illustrates his point with a vivid word picture: *"It is like the precious oil upon the head, running down upon the beard, upon the beard of Aaron, running down on the collar of his robes"* (Ps. 133:2).

Pouring oil on the head could be an act of hospitality to a weary traveler, as it is in the twenty-third psalm: *"Thou anointest my head with oil."* But here the anointing refers not to refreshment but to power. It is not a dusty wayfarer but a priest—Aaron, first of the great priests of Israel—who anointed. The background for this is found in Leviticus 8:10, 12, where the beginnings of Israel's formal and official worship are described: *"Then Moses took the anointing oil, and anointed the tabernacle and all that was in it, and consecrated them. . . . And he poured some of the anointing oil on Aaron's head, and anointed him, to consecrate him."*

This act of anointing set Aaron aside as God's special priest with the power and authority to speak in behalf of God to the people and to speak in behalf of the people to God. Our psalmist, then, seems to be saying that family unity conveys a power like the power Aaron was given when he was anointed to be a priest of God.

The power that comes from fellowship—this is the psalmist's point. There are many aspects to it. There is, for instance, the power of belonging to a group. Our individuality leads not so much to freedom as to alienation. Our language teaches us to say *I* about ourselves and *you* to others. And this very fact of grammar encourages estrangement. Not until *I* and *you* become *we* does fellowship take place; and when it does, we find our roots, our sense of belonging. We begin to know who we are and where we fit, and that's a powerful discovery.

Family relationships are not just sentimental ideas; they are indispensable ties that keep us steady and secure amid the loneliness and uncertainty of life. Grandparents, aunts and uncles, parents, brothers and sisters play a very special part in our maturing. They show us something of where we have come from and what we will be. They are instruments of heredity and environment used by God to shape us for his purposes.

The power of finding purpose is another aspect of the power of fellowship. What we do with our lives will be determined largely by three things: our abilities, our opportunities, and our interests. All three of these are closely linked to the home and family in which we are raised. Where our abilities are discovered, nurtured, and appreciated, it is easier for us to find direction and purpose in life. Strong family ties, deep commitments to the welfare of each member, are literally a gift of God, a powerful anointing of his Spirit as we seek to find useful and noble ways to live our lives for him.

Power can come from fellowship. The greatest aspect of this power is the power of experiencing grace. Fellowship-fine fellowship—within a family does not depend on perfection but on forgiveness. When a family functions as it should there is full acceptance of each member not because of what he is but in spite of what he is. This acceptance, this grace, is the most powerful ingredient known to man. It sets us free from our frustration over what we are not and from our pretenses about what we are. It liberates us for love, for worship, for service. And that's a powerful liberation.

The Blessing of Fellowship

"Behold, how good and pleasant it is when brothers dwell in unity! . . . It is like the dew of Hermon, which falls on the mountains of Zion! For there the Lord has commanded the blessing, life for evermore" (Ps. 133:1, 3). The oil of anointing is a symbol of the power that comes from fellowship; the dew that refreshes Zion's hills is a picture of the blessing that comes from fellowship.

No one who has ever known the gnawing pangs of loneliness needs illustrations of this blessing. His own experience is all too clear—and painful. Helping us cope with discouragement is a choice blessing that fellowship provides. Any problem seems worse when there is no one who understands and cares. When we go it alone our perspective becomes so distorted that anything we suffer is blown up out of all proportion. Friends within our family are irreplaceable at such times.

Helping us to enjoy our successes is another blessing our families can provide. Good news is always enjoyed more when shared with loved ones. Secret engagements and hidden marriages are excruciating experiences. To have to hush up our high moments when we want to broadcast them is a profound form of suffering. Part of a family's function is to shoulder one end of our burdens and to share the delight of our blessings.

Robert Frost said, "Home is the place where when you have to go there, They have to take you in" *(The*

Death of the Hired Man). It is that, and a whole lot more. It is a center of fellowship, where families can be friends, where power and blessing abound.

Helping us to celebrate God's love is the chief blessing our families can give us. The unity that our psalmist calls *"good and pleasant"* is as much dependent on God as was the anointing oil that made Aaron a priest or the dew that watered Zion when there was no rain. Only as we know how much God loves each of us can we begin to know how to love each other.

Friendly families are not those where there are no differences or disagreements but those where God's love provides the strong glue that binds them together whatever the differences may be. Families can be friends but only when true love takes charge. The Bible says this love comes from God. Have you found any better source?

PRAYER: Help us, Heavenly Father, to stop, look, and listen. Help us to stop quarreling and competing, comparing and rejecting, rebelling or abusing. Help us to look—to look at each other as we are: persons not things, relatives not enemies, a family not a bunch of isolated individuals. Help us to listen: to listen to each other, with full respect and appreciation for what you are making the other person to be; to listen to you for fresh thoughts on love when our ideas have failed and our attempts at love turned sour. Oil and dew you used as comparisons of your kind of love. Ours is more like sand and gravel. Forgive us for ours, and give us more of yours. For Jesus' sake. Amen.

For further study on family unity, refer to the following Scripture passages: John 15:12–17; Ephesians 4:1–3; Hebrews 13:1–2.

9

Does Charity Begin
in Your Home?

Let brotherly love continue. Do not neglect to show hospitality to strangers, for thereby some have entertained angels unawares. Remember those who are in prison, as though in prison with them; and those who are ill—treated, since you also are in the body. Let marriage be held in honor among all, and let the marriage bed be undefiled; for God will judge the immoral and adulterous. Keep your life free from love of money, and be content with what you have; for he has said, "I will never fail you nor forsake you."

9

Does Charity Begin
in Your Home?

Hebrews 13:1–5

Ours is a needy world, filled with needy people. It takes no special insight, no access to secret information to know this. All around we see evidence that some people have greater needs than others.

Hard luck we may give as the reason, or lack of opportunity, or laziness. We know the differences are there, even though we may not be sure of the reasons. In fact, discovering the reasons for the misfortune of those around us is not nearly so important as doing what we can to ease their misfortune.

Poverty, hunger, disease, loneliness may be common companions in our world, but they must always be treated as intruders, invaders, enemies. Complacency toward them is scarcely a virtue. Neither is callousness. The example of Job's comforters was not put in the Bible for us to imitate. Yet today there are people who make the same mistake; giving easy answers to difficult problems, always blaming hardship on the people who are suffering. "They deserve what's coming to them." "If they weren't so lazy, they wouldn't be so poor." "Serves them right, considering the way they live."

At times these analyses may be accurate, but they are never right. Never right, because the attitude behind them lacks concern and compassion. Because it is harsh and vindictive it contains no hope of help or healing.

Fortunately, there have always been numbers of people in the world in whose veins the milk of kindness has not turned sour. They want to help. But as the problems of poverty and hunger, of drugs and alcohol, of crime and delinquency have mounted, we have looked more and more to our governments to solve them. Governments should be involved. One of the functions of government, as the Preamble of the United States Constitution has it, is "to promote the general welfare."

Private associations and church agencies have consistently made generous contributions toward meeting the needs of people. Who can calculate the amount of good done by the Salvation Army, the YMCA, Alcoholics Anonymous, the March of Dimes, to name only a handful?

The point I want to make is simple and direct: the family ought to play a key part in helping to deal with this huge backlog of human need. Indirect involvement through taxes paid to government or contributions given to private agencies is no substitute for personal concern.

In giving closing words of advice to his fellow Christians, the author of Hebrews describes three areas of possible ministry for our homes. In fact, he does more than describe—he commands. His first command: *"Let brotherly love continue."* His second command: *"Do not neglect to show hospitality to strangers."* His

third command: *"Remember those who are in prison
. . . and those who are ill-treated"* (Heb. 13:1–3). Drop
a pebble in a pond and watch the expanding rings
enlarge until they touch the edge. Just so Christian love
has this expansive quality that reaches out in
ever-widening circles to those around us.

"Charity begins at home." This old proverb has a
wise point. We should not get so busy helping others
that we are blind to the needs of our own family. But
here I'd like to give another emphasis. "Charity begins
at home" ought to mean that our homes become
centers of service, stations of concern that reach out to
minister to the needs of others.

Love for Brothers

Picture the situation in the early church. As the
apostles trekked from town to town preaching the good
news that God had entered human experience in Jesus
Christ, many people believed—both Jews and Gentiles.
Sometimes whole families *"turned to God from idols, to
serve a living and true God, and to wait for his Son
from heaven"* (1 Thess. 1:9–10). At other times only
one person in the family responded to the gospel in
repentance and faith.

When this happened the results were dire. His family
would disown him; his employer would dismiss him; his
friends would reject him. His lifelines—social, financial,
emotional—would be cut off.

Then an amazing thing happened. He found that
other Christians began to treat him as though he were
part of their family. His name was different from theirs,
and so perhaps were his race and former religion. His
habits, speech, and culture may have seemed strange.

But he with them had met the Master and been captured by his grace. That made all the difference. Now they loved him like a brother.

Brotherly love, *philadelphia,* is what the Greek language called this new relationship. Christian clans were formed where the new ties of the Spirit were stronger than the old ties of blood. *"Let brotherly love continue"* is the command. Don't let it pale and fade after the newness wears off. When the excitement flags and the romance of this relationship wanes, don't let your deep commitment to each other in Christ grow stale. Let increasing familiarity breed concern not contempt. *"Let brotherly love continue."*

Our situation today may lack some of the drama of the early church, but the need still remains. Many Christians still feel alone, alienated from their families because of their faith. Others are open to the Christian message if only they could experience it in a context of love and acceptance.

What better place for this to happen than within a Christian family? Is there someone you know whom you can take in as a member of your clan? Someone to whom your cupboard, your home, your heart would be open whenever he needed you? Perhaps your teenage young people have a friend whose home situation is unhappy. Can you help? Perhaps you know an unmarried person at work who has no relatives nearby. What can your family do to ease that loneliness? Charity can begin in your home as you share its love and warmth with others.

Love for Strangers

The early church not only formed new clans, they

extended hospitality to strangers. Their homes were open to wayfarers who shared their Christian faith. Hotels and inns were scarce and inhospitable. Travelers, especially the itinerant preachers and evangelists or the Christians journeying from city to city on business, longed to spend nights or take meals with those who had committed their lives to Christ. Eager they were to catch up on the news of what God had done lately in the communities they were visiting. For the first hundred years or more, churches met in homes, so that Christian hospitality and Christian worship went hand in hand.

They should go together. What better opportunity do we have to show what Christ means to us than to invite people into the center of our family circle and let them see how and why we live?

It's not only the poor and downtrodden who are encouraged by our hospitality. It is anyone who likes people and wants to know them better. It is anyone who finds himself away from home and longs for a warmer fellowship than casual contacts can provide. Henrietta Mears, a great Christian leader and Bible teacher, was a gracious, outgoing person who radiated concern for others. Once I asked her how she had developed this concern. She told me that her father often carried on long conversations with salesmen and other unknown visitors who stopped at their home. When his children asked him why, his reply was profound: "You'll never meet anyone who is not lonely."

Does charity begin in your home when it comes to hospitality? What lessons of love and grace to others are being taught within your walls?

Love for the Needy

But some people, even those who are Christians, may be worse off than the strangers. The expanding circles of love must reach beyond love for the brother and beyond love for the stranger to love for the needy, whatever his need.

The third command in Hebrews makes this clear: *"Remember those who are in prison, as though in prison with them; and those who are ill-treated, since you also are in the body"* (Heb. 13:3). In those early days of the church many Christians knew the pangs of persecution. Arrested on trumped-up charges, they could be cruelly beaten, publicly abused, or harshly imprisoned. Empathy with them is to be expressed because all of us have the same potential for suffering. Our fleshly frailty is part of our human lot. Pain comes easily to all of us. We need to remember this with special care in times when suffering has passed us by.

Part of the concern of every Christian home should be for our brethren whose lines have fallen in hard places. Today as we enjoy a measure of comfort and security, others who belong to us in Christ do not. Regularly within our families, in our conversation, in our giving, in our labors, and in prayers these needy brethren must be our concern.

The family that makes charity its way of life begins to discover that it gains more than it gives. Welcoming strangers may mean entertaining angels without knowing it. If love is the law of life, it is good, literally good, for us to love. Strength and support come from treating fellow Christians as blood brothers. Blessing and encouragement are to be found in enlarging the family circle from time to time to include strangers, who bring their own gifts, their own beauty, their own faith and love to our homes.

Reaching out to the oppressed and desperate links us to God's own way of loving, for it was to our oppression and despair that he came in Jesus Christ (2 Cor. 8—9). Charity began in God's heavenly home but it did not end there. His charity reached to the furthest edges of human need. And so should ours.

PRAYER: Loving Father, show us the little ways that we can live in love. The glamorous and dramatic approaches are easier for us to see. Keep us loving when we want to quit. Nudge our love to reach out further when we are tempted to love only the attractive. Forgive us if we have been more concerned that our youngsters learn spelling, arithmetic, or baseball than concern for others. If manners have become more important than kindness, if polite speech has been stressed more than gracious deeds, if poise has outranked involvement, then let us learn from Jesus Christ what true Christianity really is. In his name. Amen.

For further study on how charity can begin in your home, refer to the following Scripture passages: Leviticus 19:17—18; Matthew 22:37—40; Matthew 25:31—40; Ephesians 6:9—10; 1 John 4:19—21.

10

How Good Is the School under Your Roof?

"Hear, O Israel: The Lord our God is one Lord; and you shall love the Lord your God with all your heart, and with all your soul, and with all your might. And these words which I command you this day shall be upon your heart; and you shall teach them diligently to your children, and shall talk of them when you sit in your house, and when you walk by the way, and when you lie down, and when you rise."

10

How Good Is the School under Your Roof?

Deuteronomy 6:4–7

What is the most influential school in the world? A fine file of names marches across our mind when we hear that question. Eton and Harrow, Groton and Exeter to name a few top prep schools. Oxford, Cambridge, St. Andrews, the Sorbonne, Harvard, Yale, Stanford to mention a handful of the great universities.

What we often overlook when we think of influential centers of education is that much of what we learn for life we learn as toddlers. A good bit of research in recent years has underscored this. Our basic intelligence, our capacity to understand and solve problems together with our understanding of language and how to use it, is largely determined before we ever darken the door of a school. Long before we throw our first paper wad or spill our first inkwell, what we will become intellectually is well on the way to being decided.

It is obvious, then, that in terms of depth of impression and breadth of influence, no school, whether large, ancient, or prestigious, public or private, can compete with the home. This is a scary thought. Almost before we know it, our youngsters are on their way to school. Not to begin their education, but to put the finishing touches on it. To be sure, they will garner away bushels of information during the sixteen years of school and college training. But their ability to sift this information and to put it to good use is almost entirely shaped before they learn to read and write.

Their value system has already shown considerable growth. What they feel about themselves and their behavior, what they believe about right and wrong, what they think about God and his purposes have had a quiet yet lasting development. The home is a center of education. Our question is not, "Is there a school under your roof?" We take for granted there is, if there are people living together. The real question is, "How good is the school that's under your roof?"

The Bible offers good help here as it has in the other questions we have raised. It reminds us that our homes are centers of worship, where daily we express and demonstrate our dependence upon God. It provides encouragement for families to be friends and to turn our homes into centers of fellowship, with all the power and blessing that fellowship can bring to our lives. Centers of service reaching out in God's name to the lonely and the needy are also what our homes are to be. Governments and social agencies have their responsibilities, but we cannot delegate all of ours to them. There is no satisfying way to love by proxy. We ourselves as persons and families must be involved.

If you think all of this talk about the home as a center is putting a terrifying amount of responsibility on the home, you're right. But this is just what the Bible does with its stress on the family as a basic social unit formed by God and charged to work his will.

Sound education is part of that will. Listen to the commandment laid upon every man of Israel: *"Hear therefore, O Israel, and be careful to do them; that it may go well with you, and that you may multiply greatly, as the Lord, the God of your fathers, has promised you, in a land flowing with milk and honey."* Then come the contents of this crucial command. *"Hear, O Israel: The Lord our God is one Lord; and you shall love the Lord your God with all your heart and with all your soul, and with all your might. And these words which I command you this day shall be upon your heart; and you shall teach them diligently to your children, and shall talk of them when you sit in your house, and when you walk by the way, and when you lie down, and when you rise"* (Deut. 6:3–7).

The Contents of the Course

"And you shall teach them diligently to your children"—these words are the charter for all Christian education, Christian education which centers in our homes. Like most education, our subject can be divided into two parts—what is being taught and how the teaching is carried on. In other words the content of the course and the nature of the instructing.

"Hear, O Israel: The Lord our God is one Lord." This simple yet profound statement contains the essence of what we ought to teach our children: the unique character of God. The word *Lord* is really God's personal name, Yahweh or Jehovah. This name was so

sacred that the Jews were reluctant to pronounce it, lest by chance they break the commandment that warned them not to take it in vain. When we call God *Lord* as the Old Testament names him, we are acclaiming his saving power.

Behind this name lies the whole account of the Exodus. A people bound in slavery he rescued. All that they needed he provided—guidance, sustenance, protection. Their enemies he put to flight; their fears he calmed; their lives he governed. The gods of Egypt and Canaan were toppled by his powers, and the foolish superstitions of those people were exposed. Israel's God was a Savior, a Rescuer, who because of his unmeasured love snatched his people from bondage and led them on the high road to life and liberty.

"The Lord our God is one Lord." The unity of God is to be stressed in our family education as well as his saving power. Our lives are ruled not by many gods but by one. We take this for granted in Western civilization because our biblical faith has left such a firm stamp on all of our thinking.

Put yourself back in those ancient days when every natural force was a separate god: sun, moon, stars, rain, drought, wind, sea, earth. Almost every human need had to be dealt with by a different deity. You practically had to have a directory, like the yellow pages of our phone book, to practice your religion. Life was fragmented, and you felt yourself to be at the mercy of the elements that used you without necessarily caring for you.

The revelation of the one, true God brought unity to life. And comfort, too, because he entered into covenant relations with his people. *"Our God"* Israel's children were taught to call him. No impersonal force was their God. He had pledged his love and protection in a unique promise made to Abraham and affirmed to his descendants. Century after century he had demonstrated his faithfulness in keeping this promise. In a special way he belonged to Israel and they to him, though he was ruler of all the nations, even those that did not know him.

These lessons about God's unique character also stress the urgency of our response. Sound education is more than hoarding facts. It has to do with changed attitudes. Israel's people were commanded not only to know about the power and unity of God and their covenant relationship with him, they were urged to love him. *"And you shall love the Lord your God with all your heart, and with all your soul, and with all your might"* (Deut. 6:5).

Knowing who God is places terrible demands on us. This knowledge makes all of life different. It gives us a focus beyond ourselves. It calls for a basic change in our perspective. Our sense of self-sufficiency gives way to a feeling of total dependence. Complaint is replaced by appreciation. We see how much we owe God, and we are grateful.

There's a basic change in our affection. Our hearts and minds are able to look away from ourselves and fix on God. His aims and purposes, his values and concerns become increasingly important to us. We are able to invest ourselves in him, to honor his lordship, to love his people, to trust his providence.

Our attitude toward creation changes. We are not afraid of it. The terrors of superstition are gone. It is our Father who made and rules the world. We have a healthy respect, a bright-eyed admiration for what he has done. We love to study his wonders in creation. But our dark fears of the unknown give way to a bold confidence that sings, "This is my Father's world."

The Nature of the Instructing

As we teach our children about God and our response to him, we want to hear what the Bible says about how we should do it. The nature of the instructing is also spelled out. *"And these words which I command you this day shall be upon your heart"* (Deut. 6:6). Only a totally committed teacher is really going to get his points across. It's idle labor if not wicked mockery for us to try to teach our children what we do not believe and practice. Not that we are perfect, but certainly our earnest aim and endeavor must be to know and love God if we expect our children to follow suit.

The Bible also encourages us to follow a thoroughly consistent pattern of teaching. This knowledge and love of God is not an elective course to be fitted in the margins of our time and interest. It is to be the center of our lives, the prime subject of our contemplation, the chief topic of our conversation. Whether we are sitting in the house, walking in the way, preparing for bed, or getting up in the morning, it is the one true God, the Savior of his people with whom we are occupied.

This is basic education. Whatever else we teach our families. without this they are ignorant. To store countless facts and miss life's purpose is to play the fool. To acquire sharp skills and then use them emptily

114

is a form of tragedy. But if the school under your roof has God as the center of its curriculum, its teachers and pupils will be wise indeed. For they will learn of God in all his ways and works, God in all his grace and greatness. From kindergarten to graduate school they will be learning lessons about the Lord of all life. This is education at its best.

PRAYER: Wise and loving Father, you are the Teacher of us all. Help us to heed the words of your wise man who said, *"Yes, if you cry out for insight and raise your voice for understanding, if you seek it like silver and search for it as for hidden treasures; then you will understand the fear of the Lord and find the knowledge of God"* (Prov. 2:3–5). This is what we crave for ourselves and our young ones—to fear you as we ought and to know you as we want. Forgive our disbelief and ignorance. Forgive especially our slowness to see you in Jesus Christ, who came to give us your full course of instruction. Lead us into true learning through him. In his great name. Amen.

For further study on the importance of family education, refer to the following Scripture passages: Deuteronmy 31:12–13; Proverbs 22:6; 1 Timothy 4:11–16.

Conclusion

What do you believe about yourself, your marriage, your family? Remember, Israelite family life hinged upon belief in God. And so did the social life of the early Christians. Is your family on a rocky road? Perhaps your belief needs changing. This doesn't mean all problems will cease, but it does mean you'll have strength to see them through—as a family.

What rules do you operate under? How is your family's structure set up? Are all family members looked upon with dignity? If your family doesn't seem to have meaning and purpose, perhaps it's because you are playing by the wrong rules. Look to God, obey his Word, and your lives will take on fresh significance.

What ministry does your family have? Are you part of God's people sharing in God's purpose? Those who believe in Christ and obey his teachings are sent out for a life of service. Through God's people the knowledge of a Savior will reach to all the families in the world. The families of God are asked to serve, and in their service they will find God's purpose.

Is the family here to stay? Of course it is. But your family, can it stay as it is? That's the real question.

Other Books by David A. Hubbard

WHAT'S NEW?

New attitudes . . . a new life of love . . . a new sense of God's presence . . . a new access of God's power . . . a new teaching . . . a new community . . . a new relationship. This book is about the new things God is doing today — now. David Hubbard sounds a positive note of hope and authentic optimism: Our lives can be changed. God stands ready to sweep out the musty staleness of stagnant living and invigorate sagging spirits with the freshness of his presence.

Hardback—2.95

DOES THE BIBLE REALLY WORK?

David Hubbard's timely focus on the inspiration and authority of the Scriptures presents solid grounds for confidence in the Word God has given. Each chapter deals in depth with an often-asked question about the Bible: What's the message of the Bible? What's so different about it? What's the Bible's main theme? Is the Bible really God's Word? Can we add to the Bible in our day?

Here's real help for getting to know your Bible and making the most of its vital message in coping with day-to-day problems.

Hardback—2.95
Paperback— .95

Other Books of Interest to the Inquiring Reader

PROMISES TO PETER

by Charlie W. Shedd

Building a bridge from parent to child is the key to happy relationships and relaxed communication within the family. Choosing from several promises made to his son, Peter, on the day of his birth, Charlie Shedd selects three as all-important:

- The promise of *Growing Self-Government*
- The promise of *Lessons in How to Love*
- The promise to teach and demonstrate the *Dignity of Work*

Over 50,000 in print   Hardback—3.95

EVERY CHILD HAS TWO FATHERS

by Samuel Southard

Fathers are special people. In this very personal book the author tells how his two daughters discovered both their fathers — God and Sam Southard — and what he learned about fatherhood in the process.

As his girls grew up, Sam Southard kept a diary of their questions about life, God, and right and wrong, as well as his answers to them. This tender account of moral development makes a helpful book for all parents of eagerly questioning children.

Hardback—2.95

RISK AND CHANCE IN MARRIAGE

by Bernard Harnik

Dealing with case studies and illustrations from his own professional counseling, Dr. Harnik delves into marriage in a unique way. He pinpoints many of the problems and pitfalls experienced even in healthy marriages and in so doing suggests practical methods of dealing with these everyday situations. A challenging handbook on marital happiness.

Hardback—4.95